STEAM
AHEAD

EXPERIMENT WITH

ENGINEERING

SCIENCE

Brimming with creative inspiration, how-to projects, and useful information to enrich your everyday life, quarto.com is a favorite destination for those pursuing their interests and passions.

Inspiring | Educating | Creating | Entertaining

Author: Nick Arnold
Illustrator: Giulia Zoavo
Cover design: Sarah Andrews
Design: Starry Dog Books Ltd, Victoria Kimonidou
Editorial: Starry Dog Books Ltd, William Petty
Consultant: Pete Robinson
Creative Director: Malena Stojic
Group Publisher: Maxime Boucknooghe

First published in 2022 by QEB Publishing,
an imprint of The Quarto Group.
100 Cummings Center, Suite 265D Beverly, MA 01915, USA.
T (978) 282-9590 F (978) 283-2742
www.quarto.com

A CIP record for this book is available from the Library of Congress.

ISBN 978-0-7112-7895-0

Manufactured in Guangdong, China TT012022

9 8 7 6 5 4 3 2 1

MIX
Paper from
responsible sources
FSC® C016973
www.fsc.org

Picture credits
All photographs by Starry Dog Books
with the exception of the following:

SHUTTERSTOCK
12-13 Olga Danylenko; 23 maimu; 23 b/g Peshkova; 29 EvgeniiAnd; 31 litchima; 36 b/g zffoto; 36-37 b/g primopiano; 40-41 b/g primopiano; 42-43 b/g Det-anan; 44-45 b/g sumroeng chinnapan; 49 hxdbzxy; 50-51 b/g FREEPIK2; 51 BonNontawat; 54-55 b/g stockphoto-graf; 56-57 b/g sumroeng chinnapan; 58-59 b/g Bildagentur Zoonar GmbH; 64-65 b/g Mike Pellinni; 66-67 b/g iva; 69 Sandeep Gore; 71 Bloomicon; 71 b/g slava17; 71 Art studio G; 73 Chesky; 73 b/g Marina_D; 74-75 b/g sdecoret; 76 GrashAlex; 76-77 b/g Ursatii;

STEAM AHEAD

EXPERIMENT WITH

ENGINEERING SCIENCE

Nick Arnold

QEB

CONTENTS

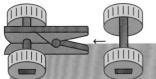

CHAPTER 4: GET A MOVE ON!

CHAPTER 5: TESTING TOMORROW

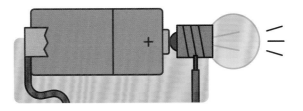

INTRODUCTION

Engineers are the brains behind everything from super-tall skyscrapers to cool computers, and the secret of their success is science. You don't need to be a science genius to follow in their footsteps. All you need are a few fun experiments...

CHAPTER 1:
BUILD IT OR BREAK IT

shows you how to build solid structures. Then have fun testing their strength by trying to knock them down!

CHAPTER 2:
MECHANICAL MARVELS

looks at the basic mechanics hidden inside some mighty machines, and the simple scientific ideas behind them.

CHAPTER 3:
ENERGY ENGINES

conducts some powerful experiments to prove that energy is the answer to getting things done!

CHAPTER 4:
GET A MOVE ON!

looks at how to build speedy machines that will get you from A to B when you're in a hurry.

CHAPTER 5:
TESTING TOMORROW

explores sustainable energy sources and other exciting engineering challenges for the future!

Golden rules
FOR SENSIBLE SCIENTISTS

Rule 1
BE ORGANIZED!

Before you start an experiment, read the instructions and make sure you have everything you need at hand.

Look out for the handy hints in circles—they will help to make the experiments work.

Rule 2
BE SAFE!

Ask for adult help wherever you see this symbol. Always follow the advice in the red WARNING! boxes. Never experiment with flames, mains electricity, or gas. Younger children will need adult help using scissors.

ASK AN ADULT

WARNING! Water may spill at stage 4.

Rule 3
BE TIDY!

Start and finish with a clean and tidy working area. Look out for the yellow MESS WARNING! boxes and follow the advice given.

⚠ MESS WARNING! Food coloring stains—wear old clothes!

THINK GREEN AND RECYCLE!

Many of the projects in this book provide a great way to recycle plastic and cardboard items; wherever possible, try to find the items you need at home rather than buying new products. When you have finished, recycle any plastic or cardboard items to keep them out of landfills.

You can try these experiments in any order, but the scientific explanations make more sense if you tackle them in the order they appear in this book.

You can find out about the science words in **bold** in the glossary on pages 78-79.

CHAPTER 1: BUILD IT OR BREAK IT

BUILD A GUMMY HOUSE

Here's how to build a super-strong structure shaped like a house using just a few candies and some sticks. Have fun testing its strength!

1 Take four wooden toothpicks and push a gummy candy onto each end of all four sticks.

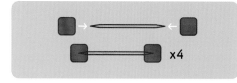

2 Push eight more toothpicks into the gummy candies to make a cube, as shown. These are the walls of your house.

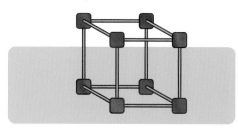

3 To test the strength of the walls, lay a ruler across the sticks and place a 2-ounce weight on top. What happens to the upright sticks?

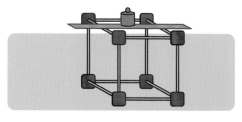

4 To make the roof, remove the top square from the cube. Push four toothpicks into the corner candies of this square and hold them in place with another candy. Balance the weight on top. Is the structure strong enough to support the weight?

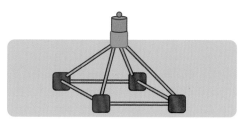

5 Replace the roof on the cube. Then balance the weight on top. What do you notice? To make it stronger, add some extra candies and toothpicks as shown, and test the strength again.

Extra candies (blue)   Extra toothpicks (blue)

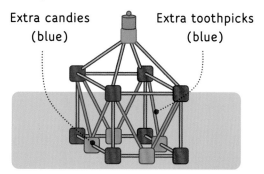

You will need...

- Toothpicks
- Gummy candies
- Short ruler
- 2 ounce weight

2oz

The Science: GRAVITY AND SHAPES

Engineers build models to test how forces affect their designs. When you tested the strength of the walls, gravity pulled the weight down until the angles between the sticks changed and the cube buckled. But with the roof, the length of the leaning sticks resisted gravity and the angles between the sticks didn't change. Triangles are a super-strong shape for structures.

DID YOU KNOW?

The Eiffel Tower in Paris is made of iron girders arranged in triangles. On hot days, the girders swell and the tower grows 6 inches taller!

At steps 4, 5, and 6, you may need to hold the weight loosely in place so it doesn't fall off.

WATER UNDER THE BRIDGE

Where would we be without bridges? In the water! Find out how to build and test the strength of four different bridge designs.

1 Draw a line down the middle of two pieces of thick printer-size cardstock. Cut along the lines to make four cardstock rectangles.

x2

2 Place two boxes upside down and 9 inches apart. Spread the lid flaps out as shown.

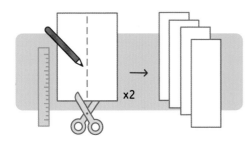

9 in

3 Use tape to secure the flaps to the surface.

4 Lay a cardstock rectangle between the two boxes to form a bridge.

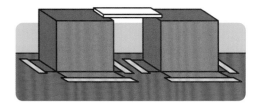

5 Place a small weight on your bridge. Keep adding more weights until the bridge collapses. How many weights did it take to collapse the bridge? Weigh each weight and note down their combined weight.

You will need...

- Ruler
- Pencil
- Two pieces of thick printer-size cardstock
- Scissors
- Two large cardboard boxes
- Tape
- 12 identical weights such as marbles, bolts, or fruit
- Kitchen scales
- Notebook
- Shallow cardstock tray or light plastic lid

Bridge challenge:
ARRANGE THE WEIGHTS IN DIFFERENT PATTERNS

Arrange the weights in different patterns. Does the bridge last longer if you balance some weights on the ends of the bridge? Place a cardstock tray or light plastic lid on the bridge. Does the bridge collapse more quickly when the weights are on the lid or tray?

The Science:
GRAVITY AND A BRIDGE

Weight is the force of gravity pulling an object downward. Even without any extra weights, gravity pulls on the bridge. When you add weights, you increase the force of gravity until the cardstock curves down. Because the ends of the cardstock aren't secured to the boxes, the bridge collapses.

Real bridges must withstand gravity and carry the weight of people and vehicles. Long bridges often need piers at either end, and even extra piers in the middle, to support the weight.

Discover some cool engineering secrets that will help to make your bridge stronger...

6 Fold a second cardstock rectangle lengthways to make a zigzag shape, as shown. Replace the first bridge with the folded cardstock.

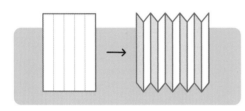

7 Repeat step 5 and note down your results.

8 Replace the folded cardstock bridge with the unfolded cardstock from step 4.

9 Bend a third length of cardstock into an arch shape. Tape its ends to the sides of the boxes, as shown, so the arch is supporting the cardstock bridge.

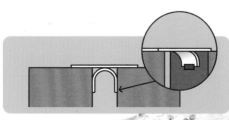

10 Repeat step 5 and note down your results.

11 Now try putting the folded cardstock bridge over the arch. Place the unfolded cardstock on top of the folded cardstock bridge to make a smooth surface.

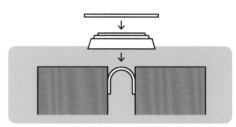

12 Repeat step 5 and note down your results. Compare your results from steps 5, 7, 10 and 12.

13 Now try making your bridge even stronger. Tape the two ends of the bridge to the tops of the boxes and tape the arch to the bridge.

DID YOU KNOW?

The Chaotianmen Bridge in China has an arch that spans 1,811 feet—that's about ⅓ mile!

The Science: STRENGTHENING A BRIDGE

The zigzag bridge has lots of triangles working side by side to withstand gravity (see page 9). The downward force of gravity travels down the sides of the triangles. The bases of the sides push against each other to resist the downward force.

An arch works in a different way. The downward force travels down the curve of the arch and pushes against the sides of the boxes.

Just like a real engineer, you tested the effects of gravity on different bridge designs. The strongest design at step 11 combined the strength of many triangles with the support provided by the arch.

You could decorate your bridge with colored pens and make a model river from a length of aluminum foil.

IT'S TOUGH AT THE TOP

A big building needs a really BIG roof. But how can you design one that won't crush the building? Let's find out...

1 Place a box upside down on the floor. Put a 2.2-pound weight on the box. What happens to the sides of the box?

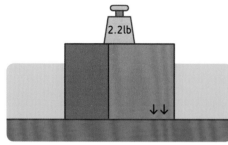

2 Now take a bowl and place it upside down on the box. Put the weight on top of the bowl. What happens to the sides of the box this time?

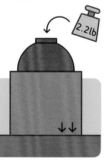

3 Repeat step 2, but this time stand four cardboard tubes on the box and rest the bowl on the tubes.

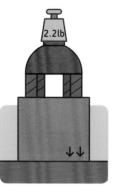

The bowl should be as wide as the base of the box, or a little less wide.

You will need...

- Cardboard box
- 4 cardboard tubes (eg toilet roll tubes)
- 2.2-pound weight
- Plastic or paper bowl

2.2lb

You could use a 2.2-pound bag of sugar instead of a weight.

The Science: DOMES AND PILLARS

The box represents a building with four thin walls. In step 1, the weight boosts the force of gravity pulling on the roof. As the roof bows, it pulls the walls inward. If the weight was heavier, the walls would collapse.

The bowl is a dome, similar to the domed roofs of many famous buildings. As in an arch, the force of gravity is sent down the dome's curved sides. In step 2, since the force is evenly spread and falls on the top of the walls, the walls themselves aren't pulled in any direction.

In step 3, the tubes act like pillars. Just like the dome, they transmit the force of gravity downward. Since the force presses evenly on the top of the sides of the tubes, they stay straight. Engineers use pillars to hold up heavy roofs without the need for thick walls. They also use pillars to support a dome or a big roof.

DID YOU KNOW?

The huge dome of the Pantheon, an Ancient Roman temple built 1,900 years ago, was the widest in the world until the 19th century.

TUNNEL TESTERS

If you can't get over it, just go under it!
A tunnel must be the right shape to withstand
the weight of earth above it. Have fun testing
the strength of three tunnel designs.

WARNING!
Soil contains bacteria.
Bandage any cuts on your
hands and wear gloves
before you touch soil.

1 Take three cardboard tubes and
mark them A, B, and C.

2 Squash tube A flat and stand on
it. Press the two folds to make
the edges sharp.

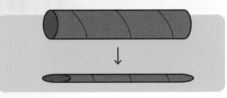

3 Fold the tube lengthways and
stand on it again to make the
edges sharp. Open the tube up.
It will now be squarish instead
of round.

4 Cut Tube B lengthways and
open it to make a cardboard
rectangle, with the outside
facing up. Using a ruler, fold
into thirds as shown, then tape
edge 1 to edge 2 to make a
triangular tube.

Edge 1   Edge 2

5 Measure tube A's tunnel entrance
height, then dig a trench twice
this depth and lay the tube in
it. Cover the tube with soil and
place a 1.1-pound weight on
top. After 10 minutes, dig up
the tube. How has its
shape changed?

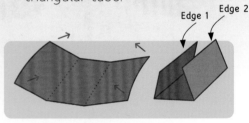

- 3 paper towel tubes
- Marker
- Scissors
- Ruler
- Wide tape
- Gloves

- Small spade, trowel, or tablespoon
- Soil or sand
- 1.1-pound weight (such as a small bag of flour)

The Science: THE SHAPE OF TUNNELS

In this experiment, the force of gravity pressing on each tunnel is boosted by the 1.1-pound weight and the weight of the soil. Like a dome or an arch, the rounded top of tube C deals best with the downward force of gravity. The soil under the tubes pushes back, and the rounded base of tube C is best suited to dealing with this pressure from below. That's why real tunnels are often circular in cross-section rather than square or rectangular.

6 Repeat step 5 for tubes B and C. Make sure you bury them at the same depth as tube A. This will ensure that the experiment is a fair test of each tunnel's strength.

The soil should be fairly dry and free from stones. You could also try this project using sand on a beach.

Cheesy challenge:

Can you bore through a block of cheese using a corkscrew (the type without arms)? Like a corkscrew, real hole-boring machines rotate and use pressure to get through rock.

NO-GO WITH THE FLOW

Water goes where it flows. Your mission is to build a dam to stop it—using engineering!

ASK AN ADULT

1 Take a 4-pint plastic milk bottle and use a ruler and pen to draw lines across the neck end and along its length, as shown. Ask an adult to cut along the lines using sharp scissors.

4 Put both bottles on a table and overlap the open ends by about 1 inch. Prop the end without the spillway on a couple of books. Tape along the join inside and outside with duct tape. You have made a dam!

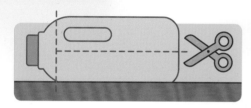

ASK AN ADULT

2 Repeat with a second 4-pint milk bottle.

3 Cut a small semi-circle out of the flat end of one of the bottles. This is your spillway.

The Science: WATER FLOW AND DAMS

When you poured the water slowly, it built up in the flat bottle, forming a reservoir. When you increased the flow of water, it spilled over the semi-circular dip, or spillway. Real dams have curved sides. The curve works like a dome or arch to withstand the force of the water.

5 Outside, support the sloping end on a mound of earth. Then slowly pour water into the sloping channel so it flows toward the spillway end, where the flow is stopped. What happens when you increase the flow of water?

Make a setting for your dam by adding a few trees and boulders using twigs and stones.

SHAKE, RATTLE, AND ROLL

Engineers need to check that new buildings are earthquake-proof. It's time for an earth-shaking experiment...

1 Place four pencils on a surface. Lay four more pencils crossways over the top of the first pencils, then add another four pencils facing the same direction as the bottom pencils.

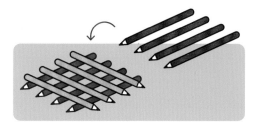

2 Pour some rice grains into a shallow box until the rice is about 1 inch deep.

3 Cut out a 4 x 4 inch square of cardboard and lay it on the rice. Stand the shallow box on the pencils. Build an 8-inch tall tower from toy building bricks or small boxes and place it on the cardboard.

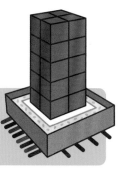

4 Be an earthquake! Shake the shallow box from side to side and note how easily the tower falls over.

5 Cut an 8 x 16 inch rectangle of cardboard. Fold it in quarters as shown. Tape A to B to make a hollow tower, then tape a straw to each corner.

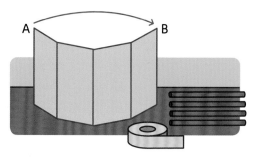

6 Cut a 4.5 x 4.5 inch square of polystyrene. Push four toothpicks into the polystyrene ¼ inch in from each corner. Slide the tower straws over the toothpicks.

7 Take the cardboard square out of the box and put in the polystyrene square and tower. Now be an earthquake again! Shake the shallow box from side to side. What happens this time?

You will need...

- 12 pencils
- Rice
- Shallow box
- Ruler
- Scissors
- Cardboard
- Toy building bricks or small boxes
- Card
- Wide tape
- 4 drinking straws
- Polystyrene tile or pizza base
- 4 toothpicks

The Science: EARTHQUAKE ENGINEERING

Earthquakes occur when one tectonic plate suddenly moves against another. The shockwaves make the soil behave like a liquid (represented by your rice box), and the waves make any buildings shake. Buildings are designed to withstand the downward force of gravity, but the sideways shake of an earthquake can topple them.

You might think that heavier buildings, such as the toy brick tower, would stand up better than light buildings, but this isn't always the case. Your drinking-straw tower has two features used by real engineers to protect against earthquakes:

1 A soft base that soaks up shockwaves rather than passing them up into the walls.

2 A flexible frame and walls that soak up and move with the shockwaves.

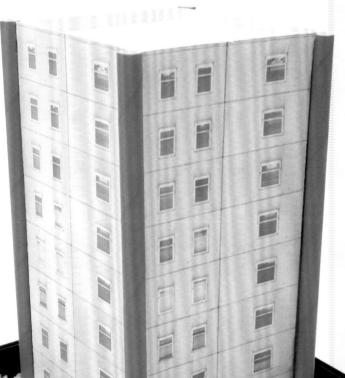

If you don't have a polystyrene tile, you could stick 2 to 3 pieces of thick cardboard together to make a thick cardboard tile.

WHAT GOES UP MUST COME DOWN

Engineers used to use wrecking balls to knock structures down. Find out how to make your own wrecking ball. Then get wrecking!

1 Cut 20 feet of twine. Loop the twine through the pull ring so that two equal lengths of twine hang from the ring.

ASK AN ADULT

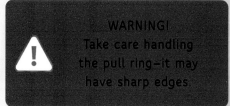

2 Tie the two free ends of twine together to make a loop. Duct-tape the knot to the ball, then use pieces of duct tape to secure the lengths of twine to the ball as shown.

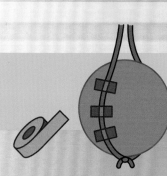

3 Tightly twist the two lengths of the twine at the top of the ball, and wind a piece of duct tape around them.

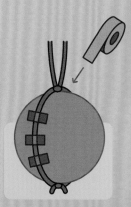

4 Ask an adult to hammer a drawing pin or picture pin into the top of a doorframe and place the ring over it so that the ball swings freely.

ASK AN ADULT

5 Build a tower from toy blocks. Then swing your wrecking ball and knock the tower down!

Super-strong tower challenge:

Place a 2.2-pound weight at the bottom of a tall cardboard box. Does this make the box easier or harder to knock over?

- Ring pull from an aluminum can
- Tape measure
- 20 feet string
- Scissors
- Ball
- Duct tape
- Toy building blocks
- Tall cardboard box
- 2.2 pound weight

The Science:
MASS, MOMENTUM, AND LATERAL FORCE

Your ball and twine works like a wrecking ball. During the 1900s, engineers used wrecking balls to demolish large concrete or brick buildings. Today, it's more usual for them to use machines or explosives.

A wrecking ball is usually attached to a chain and hung from a crane. It can either be dropped on a building or swung sideways. Either way, the ball's force depends on its momentum. The ball's momentum, in turn, depends on its mass and speed.

On pages 20-21 you discovered how an earthquake may knock buildings down by sideways or lateral force, and a wrecking ball works in the same way.

DID YOU KNOW?

The largest wrecking balls were made from steel that was squeezed when almost red hot. This made the steel very heavy. Such balls weighed about 6 tons—that's more than FOUR small cars!

RAMP UP THE SCIENCE!

Lifting can be hard work, but a ramp can make light work of it. Find out how! Then turn the page for some more ramp science...

1 Ask an adult to make two holes on opposite sides of a paper cup, just under the rim.

ASK AN ADULT

2 Cut a piece of string the same length as a plank of wood. Thread one end of the string through the holes in the cup, make a loop, and tie a knot.

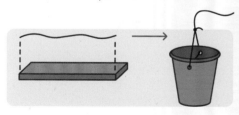

3 Wrap the other end of the string around an orange, knot the string, and tape it in place. Repeat several times.

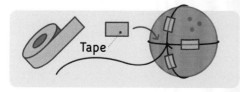
Tape

4 Put a few books on the edge of a worktop and prop the plank on them as shown. Place the orange at the other end of the plank and dangle the cup over the edge.

You will need...

- Sharp pencil
- Paper cup
- Plank of wood
- Scissors
- String
- Orange
- Duct tape
- Books
- Small coins
- Kitchen scales
- Notebook and pencil
- Tape
- Cooking oil
- Kitchen towel

If you don't have any large books to prop up the plank, you could use an upside-down box instead.

5 One by one, add some coins to the cup until the orange moves up the ramp. Weigh the orange and note down its weight. Weigh the coins and note down their weight.

6 Stick two lines of tape down the middle of the plank. Pour a little cooking oil onto a piece of kitchen paper and smear the tape with the oil. Repeat step 5. What do you notice?

The Science:
RAMPS AND FRICTION

When you lift the orange you're fighting against gravity. Your plank is a ramp—a simple lifting machine used by engineers. Using a ramp takes the same total effort as raising the load without one, but the effort is spread over a longer distance (the ramp), so you need less effort at any one moment. This makes the work easier.

As the orange travels up the ramp, the force of friction resists its movement and slows it down. The cooking oil reduces friction and reduces the effort needed. That's why, at step 6, you needed fewer coins to move the orange.

CUTTING-EDGE TECHNOLOGY

You can make ramps into tools.
In fact, you can even chop with them...

1 Fold a printer-size sheet of cardstock in half and then half again, as shown.

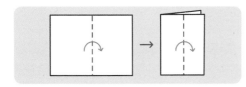

2 Fold the card over and press along the fold with a ruler to make the crease sharp.

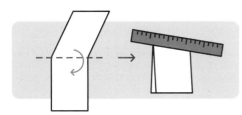

3 Open the last fold and turn over the ends by ½ inch.

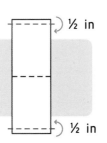

½ in

½ in

4 Turn the cardstock over and again fold the ends over by ½ inch.

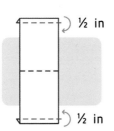

½ in

½ in

5 Fold the ends in again by ½ inch, and then once again.

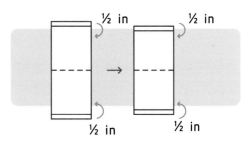

½ in   ½ in

½ in   ½ in

6 Turn the cardstock over and again fold the ends over by ½ inch.

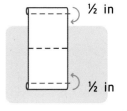

½ in

½ in

7 Press the folded sections tightly together and wrap tape around the whole shape. You've now made a wedge that you can use as a tool.

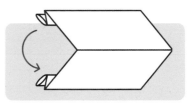

You will need...

- Printer-size sheet of cardstock
- Ruler
- Wide tape
- Butter (softened to room temperature)
- Toast—optional!
- Cardboard box
- Sheet of paper
- Sharp pencil

The Science:
WEDGES AND TOOLS

A wedge is a tool with two sloping sides. When you cut the butter with your wedge, the sharp edge concentrates the force of your push. Just like a ramp (see page 25), the sloping sides of the wedge spread your effort over a longer distance. Axes, nails, and knives are all wedge tools that work in this way.

DID YOU KNOW?

Your teeth are slightly wedge shaped. This makes it easier to bite into food.

8 Press the thin end of the wedge into some butter. Slice some off to spread on a piece of toast!

At steps 3, 4, 5, and 6, use a ruler to check that the folds are ½ in wide.

Wedge challenge:

Tape a sheet of paper over the open end of a box. Try to push the blunt end of a pencil through the paper. Then do the same using the pointed end. Which end pushes through more easily? Why do you think this is?

HOLD TIGHT!

Sloping sides are great at cutting things—and they hold things together too... hopefully!

1 Write A and B on the labels and stick one sticker to each bottle. Pour 1 cup vinegar into each bottle.

2 Place a sheet of toilet paper on a surface. Place 4 teaspoonfuls of baking powder on the sheet. Fold the sheet around the baking powder in a parcel.

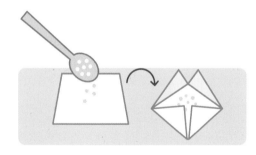

3 Tilt bottle A slightly, wedge the parcel into the neck of the bottle so it stays there, and tighten the lid.

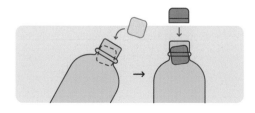

4 Turn Bottle A upside-down and then the right way up.

5 Repeat steps 3 and 4 for Bottle B, but this time stretch the balloon over the neck of the bottle instead of screwing on the lid. Give bottle B a couple of GENTLE shakes.

6 Slowly unscrew the lid of Bottle A. At what point do you notice gas or froth escaping?

You will need...

- Two identical plastic 500-ml bottles
- Sticky labels
- Marker
- Measuring jug
- Vinegar
- Funnel
- Toilet paper
- Teaspoon
- Baking powder
- Balloon

The Science:
CHEMICAL REACTION AND SCREWS

Mixing vinegar and baking powder produces a chemical reaction. The chemicals involved are the acid in vinegar and a substance called a base in baking powder. The chemical reaction makes carbon-dioxide gas. The gas pushes outward and tries to escape. Bottle A has a screw lid. A screw works like a spiral ramp—making drilling into an object easier. The gas can't push up the lid because it can only be raised by turning. The swelling of the balloon on bottle B shows how strongly the gas is pushing outward.

29

LEVERS AND LOADS

A lever is an engineering machine that lifts things—but you can also use it to catapult a ball into the air. Have fun testing your lever catapult!

1 Stand a paper cup on one end of a thin plank of wood or hardboard. Stick a drawing pin through the base of the cup to secure it to the plank. Lay a coffee can on its side and place the plank on the can, as shown.

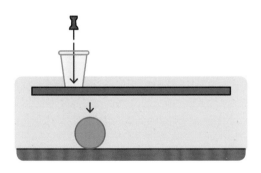

2 Ask a friend to place a table tennis ball inside the cup. Then balance the plank on the can as shown. Your helper will need to hold the cup end of the plank level.

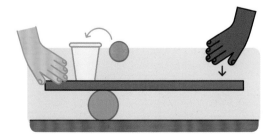

3 Now stamp on the other end of the plank. Measure how far the ball flies and make a note of the distance.

4 Repeat steps 2 and 3, but this time move the coffee can to the middle of the plank.

If you don't have a plank, you could use a wooden ruler. Balance it on a small, round container.

You will need...

- Paper cup
- Thin plank of wood or hardboard about 18 inches long
- Drawing pin
- Coffee can
- Table tennis ball
- Tape measure
- Helper

Instead of stamping, you could thump the plank down with your hand.

5 Repeat steps 2 and 3 again, but put the coffee can three-quarters of the way along the plank, close to the end that you stamp on. Compare your results at steps 3, 4, and 5.

The Science:
LEVER

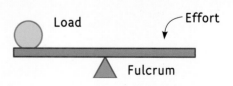

The plank in this experiment is a form of lever. The coffee can is the pivot on which the lever balances, and is called a fulcrum. Levers are simple machines that raise loads. Just like a ramp, a lever spreads the effort of lifting a load over a greater distance, which makes the task easier.

When you stamped on the lever in step 5, you used the same amount of force as in steps 3 and 4, but the ball flew farther and traveled faster because the lever was raised a greater distance.

TURNING FORCES

Wheels don't just get you from A to B;
they can be used to help lift things, too.
Take a spin to find out how it's done!

1 Cut out two cardboard discs about 1 and 3 inches in diameter. Ask an adult to make a hole in the middle of each disc with an awl. The hole should be big enough to slide a pencil through.

ASK AN ADULT

2 Cut 16 inches of string and tie one end to the middle of a pencil. Secure the knot with tape.

3 Push the ends of the pencil through the holes in the cardboard discs. Secure with tape.

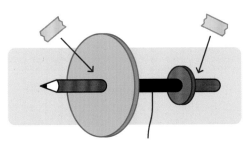

4 Fill a small plastic bottle with water. Ask an adult to make a hole in the lid with an awl, thread the string through, and secure with a knot. Screw on the lid.

5 Take two drink cartons and ask an adult to make a hole near the top of each one with an awl or sharp pencil. Ask them to enlarge the holes with scissors. Insert the ends of the pencil with the bottle attached into the holes.

ASK AN ADULT

6 Turn the large cardboard disc to wind the string around the pencil and raise the bottle. Then repeat using the small disc. Which disc turns the pencil more easily?

You will need...

- Cardboard
- Ruler
- Scissors
- Awl
- String
- Pencil
- Tape
- Small plastic bottle with screw lid (such as a food coloring bottle)
- Water
- Two drink cartons

The Science:
THE WHEEL AND FORCES

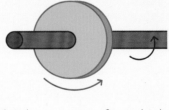

The pencil works like an axle. It turned more easily when you rotated the larger disc or wheel. That's because, like a ramp (page 25) or a lever (page 31), the large wheel spreads the effort over a larger distance.

Wheels are great for vehicles because a wheel changes the turning force of the axle into distance covered by the wheel rim. Larger wheels can cover a greater distance for the same amount of force from the axle.

PULLEY POWER

You can have the strength of two people without sweating. All you need is engineering!

1 Ask an adult to cut a 20-foot length of twine.

ASK AN ADULT

Pulley challenge:

You'll need a large plastic bottle with a lid and handle. You'll also need strong twine and a pole set up between two supports. If you don't have a suitable pole you could simply use a bannister.

Fill the bottle with water and tighten the lid. Tie the twine to the handle as shown and loop it over the pole. Lay the bottle on the floor and lift it by pulling on the twine. How many times can you loop the twine over the pole?

Why does this make lifting the bottle easier?

2 Lay two poles 24 inches apart. Tie one end of the twine to pole A as shown. Loop the twine around the poles at least three times.

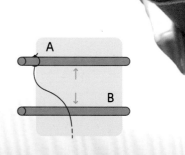

DID YOU KNOW?

According to legend the Greek scientist and engineer Archimedes (287-212 BCE) used pulleys to pull a ship onto land—all by himself!

3 Ask a friend to grip pole A. Their fists should be a good distance apart and they should not be holding any twine. Ask another friend to grip pole B.

4 Now pull on the twine while your friends try to pull the two poles apart.

The Science:
PULLEYS AND FORCE

The twine and poles form a pulley. Like a ramp, lever, and wheel, a pulley spreads your effort over a distance. This means that with a pulley, you can lift a load with less force by pulling a rope a greater distance.

Real pulleys use wheels instead of poles. As you lift a load the wheels help to support its weight. And like the poles, the wheels make the rope travel a greater distance. The more wheels you have, the less effort you need to move the load at any one time.

35

TICK, TOCK, DRIP CLOCK!

Add energy to engineering and things start to move. In this experiment, find out how dripping water can be used to power a clock!

1 Take a 2-liter plastic bottle and draw a line around it just over halfway up. Ask an adult to cut along the line.

ASK AN ADULT

2 Ask an adult to use an awl or hammer and nail to punch a ⅛ inch hole in the bottle top.

ASK AN ADULT

3 Screw the lid tightly back on the bottle. Turn the upper half of the bottle upside-down and push it into the lower half. The bottle top should now be about 4 inches from the base of the bottle.

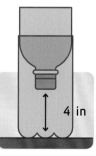

4 in

4 Pour 3 cups of water into the top half of the bottle. The water should drip into the lower half of the bottle. Mark the water level every minute until it's all gone.

5 Empty the bottle, and repeat step 4, comparing the water level with the marks you made. Why do you think the marks aren't evenly spaced?

DID YOU KNOW?

When you're 33 feet underwater, the pressure on your body is twice that of air. When you're 8,200 feet down, the water pressure on your big toe is equal to an elephant balancing on top of it.

To remove labels from a bottle, try soaking the bottle in warm, soapy water and then scrubbing the labels off.

The Science: WATER PRESSURE AND GRAVITY

Congratulations! You've made a water clock—or, if you were an Ancient Greek, a *clepsydra*. The energy to move the water comes from the pull of gravity on the water. This produces a force called water pressure.

Water pressure increases with depth, so the water dripped faster when the upper half of the bottle was full. As it emptied, the drips slowed down, so your minute marks were farther apart.

Water pressure plays an important part in engineering projects that involve water. Deep-sea machines, such as submersibles, have to be very strong to withstand the water pressure in the ocean.

UPSIDE-DOWN WATER

Everyone knows that water flows downhill. So when water flows uphill, that's against the Laws of Science—right?

> ⚠ **MESS WARNING!**
> Water will get spilled and food coloring stains hands and clothes. Put down newspaper or plastic sheeting and wear old clothes for this experiment.

1 Cut a 38-inch length of thin tubing. Use duct tape to stick one end of the tubing near the base of a 500-ml plastic bottle. The end should stick out a little over a ½ inch from the side.

↕ ½ in

2 Coil the tubing around the bottle five times. Use duct tape to secure the other end of the tubing to the neck end of the bottle. Make sure it projects a ½ inch.

The coils should be evenly spaced.

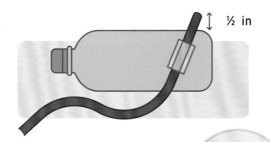

½ in

½ in

3 Use duct tape to secure the coils of tubing to the sides of the bottle.

4 Make a hole near the rim of a yogurt cup and slide the tubing through the hole.

5 Fill a bowl with water and add a few drops of food coloring. Position a second, empty bowl on some books, under the top end of the tubing.

6 Start turning the bottle and watch where the water goes. What happens if you turn the bottle the other way?

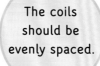

The Science:
GRAVITY, LIQUIDS, AND SCREWS

The simple pump that you've just made is called an Archimedes screw. It's named after the ancient Greek scientist and engineer Archimedes (see page 34), who wrote about it. The energy to power the pump comes from you turning the bottle, and from gravity.

When you start to turn the bottle, the end of the tube scoops water from the bowl. As you turn it some more, the water moves up the tube. This happens because the tube briefly turns downward, so gravity pulls the water down. With each turn, more water is taken into the tube and the water in the tube can move higher until it exits at the top of the tube.

Thin plastic tubing can be bought from pet shops. It's used to supply air to an aquarium.

(see page 34)

You will need...

- Tape measure
- Scissors
- Thin plastic tubing
- Duct tape
- 500-ml plastic bottle
- 2 bowls
- Water
- Food coloring
- Yogurt cup

Water can be made to flow uphill using air. Have some fun with pistons and siphons...

You will need...

- Pump from liquid soap dispenser
- 2 glasses
- Water
- Thin tubing
- Bucket
- Food coloring (optional)

1 Unscrew the pump from a soap dispenser. Wash it in clean water to remove any soap.

2 Stand two glasses next to each other and fill one with water.

3 Stand the pump in the water and position it so the dispenser overhangs the empty glass. Push the top of the pump down, and watch the water run into the empty glass.

Dispenser

Tube challenge:

Fill a sink with water and place a bucket on the floor in front of the sink. Put one end of some thin plastic tubing into the water. Take the other end, and suck out the air. As you do so, the water will move up the tube.

Keeping one end of the tube under the water, point the other end down toward the bucket. Like magic, the water will flow through the tube on its own! This is the siphon effect.

By sucking out the air you lower the air pressure in the tube. This allows water to flow up the tube. As water falls down the tube to the bucket more water is drawn up the tube.

The Science:
PISTON, VALVE, AND AIR PRESSURE

Inside the chamber are a piston, a spring, and a ball. The ball is a valve—a device that controls liquid flow. A piston is a disc on the end of a rod that moves up and down a tube.

The pump works like this:

1 As you push on the handle, this pushes down the spring and piston. The piston pushes down the ball to block the lower opening of the chamber.

2 Some air is forced from the dispenser.

3 When you release the handle, the uncoiling spring raises the piston and the ball rises. Because the air pressure is now lower in the chamber, water is drawn up the tube to fill the space.

4 When you push again on the handle, this time instead of air, water is forced from the dispenser. In this pump, the energy comes from your push and the force of air pressure.

Chamber

Tube

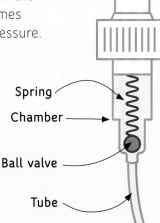

Spring

Chamber

Ball valve

Tube

You can have fun by adding different food colorings to the water.

41

GET IN GEAR...

Gears are vital parts in many machines, from clocks to cars. Find out how gears control the flow of energy by making your own gear wheel...

1 Use a compass and pen to draw a circle about 5 inches wide on a sheet of thin cardstock.

2 With the point of the compass in the same place as step 1, draw a 4-inch circle inside the first circle.

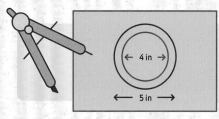

3 Draw ratchet teeth between the two lines, as shown. The teeth should all be the same size and evenly spaced. Cut out your ratchet wheel template.

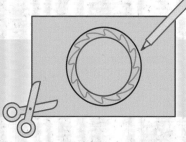

4 Place the template on a paper plate or polystyrene pizza base and draw around it, then cut out the shape. You now have a thicker, stronger ratchet wheel.

5 Push a map pin into the center of your ratchet wheel and pin it to a corkboard.

6 Copy the outline of this pawl shape onto white paper using the dimensions shown.

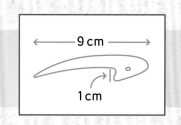

7 Cut out the pawl shape and put it on a sheet of thick cardstock. Draw around the shape and cut it out. Then cut out a 3 x 1-in cardstock rectangle.

8 Pin your cardstock pawl shape and cardstock rectangle to the cork board, as shown. Turn the gear wheel. Does it turn equally well in both directions?

You will need...

- Thin cardstock
- Ruler
- Compass
- Pen
- Scissors
- 4 map pins
- Corkboard
- Sheet of paper
- Thick cardstock
- Paper plate or polystyrene pizza base

The Science:
GEARS AND RATCHETS

Gears are vital parts in many machines—from clocks to cars. Most gear wheels can turn in both directions, but your pawl wheel is designed to only turn clockwise. You'll find ratchets in roller blinds, seat belt rollers, and mechanical clocks.

Gears transfer force when their teeth engage with the teeth of another gear or machine part. Like any other wheel, larger gear wheels turn more slowly but with greater force than smaller wheels. This means you can connect a larger gear wheel to a smaller wheel to change the force and speed of the movement.

ROCKET LAUNCH

Many machines store energy before using it. Find out how to unleash some stored energy by launching a rocket. 5... 4... 3... 2... 1... We have lift-off!

3 Slot the fins together and slide them into the slots in the tube. Secure with duct tape.

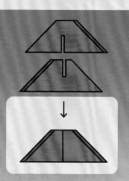

1 Cut out a 4-inch square of polystyrene or cardboard. Cut the square in half diagonally, then cut the corners off each triangle to make fins. Cut a slot in each fin, as shown.

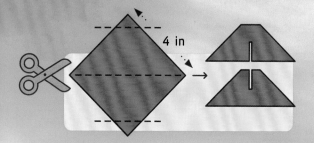

4 in

4 Cut a 5-in length of duct tape in half lengthways, and stick one half on top of the other. Use this double-thickness tape to firmly secure the elastic band to the end of the foam tube. Wrap duct tape around the tube to secure the double-thickness tape.

Double-thickness tape

2 Cut a 12-inch length of foam insulation tube. Cut four slots for the fins at one end.

5 Cut a 6-inch wide circle of thin cardstock, cut a slit to the center, and roll it into a cone. Stick it to the tube with duct tape. If you have a detergent bottle lid, stick it in the tube to make an engine.

44

You will need...

- Pen
- Ruler
- Scissors
- Polystyrene pizza base or thin cardstock
- Foam insulation tube 12 in long and 2 in wide
- Duct tape
- Wide elastic band
- Thin cardstock
- Lid of laundry detergent bottle (optional)
- Splinter-free wood, approx. 5 x 1 x 1 in
- Saw

EXPLORER 1

Energy store challenge:

Look back to page 41. What device did the pump use to store energy? Can you think of other machines that use this device?

Answer:
A spring. Springs are found in many machines including wind-up clocks.

6 Take a piece of wood about 5 x 1 x 1 inch and ask an adult to saw a small notch at one end. This will be your launch handle. Loop the elastic band over the notch and pull the rocket back so the elastic band is at full stretch. Release the band from the notch and watch your rocket shoot up into the air.

ASK AN ADULT

The Science: FUEL AND POTENTIAL ENERGY

Machines often store energy in a fuel tank. In a similar way, your rocket stores its energy in the elastic band. When you pull the elastic, the energy of your pull stretches the elastic molecules. The energy is now stored. When you release the elastic band, the stored energy turns into movement energy for your rocket.

ELECTROMAGNETIC MOTOR MACHINE

Which force can move a machine without even touching it? Let's find out...

1 Cut off about 10 feet of 22 gauge electrical wire. Wind it 30 times around a marker, then slide the pen out to leave a wire coil.

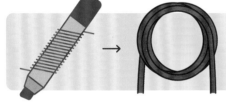

2 Wrap the ends of the wire around the coil a few times to keep the coil together.

ASK AN ADULT

3 Ask an adult to trim each end of the wire with scissors to about 2.5-3 inches long. Then ask them to strip away the plastic coating from the top half of the ends with a sharp knife.

4 Push the battery onto a blob of sticky tack and support it on each side with two larger blobs to stop it from rolling.

The eyes of the needles must be large enough for the wire to thread through.

If nothing happens, try spinning the coil in the opposite direction.

You will need...

- 22g electrical wire, about 10 feet long
- Marker
- Scissors
- Sharp knife
- Large, round 1.5 volt battery
- Sticky tack
- Two large sewing needles
- Insulating tape
- Ferrite disc magnet

The Science:
ELECTROMAGNETISM AND ELECTRIC MOTORS

The energy that turns the coil is called electromagnetism. An electric current flows from the battery through the wire and back to the battery. The current produces electric and magnetic forces, and these turn the coil into a magnet. As the coil turns, the disc magnet pushes it away. If you had removed all the plastic coating from the ends of the wire, as the coil turned further, its magnetism would have pulled on the magnet and the coil would have stopped. But by removing only half the insulating layer, you made the current pulse, repeatedly switching off the coil's magnetism. The coil has no chance to pull on the disc magnet, so it just gets pushed, and this keeps it turning.

5 Thread one end of the wire through the eye of a large needle. Repeat with the other end. Try to keep the wire and coil straight. Use insulating tape to stick the needles to the ends of the battery.

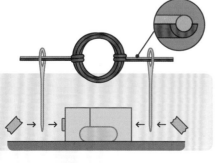

6 Tape a disc magnet to the battery, then gently spin the coil. What do you notice?

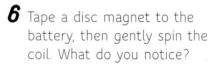
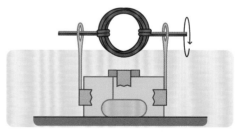

WARNING!
Magnets are a choking hazard. Keep away from small children. You must use a ferrite magnet. Other materials may be especially harmful if swallowed.

BUILD YOUR OWN CAR!

Motor engineers build their own cars, and now you can, too—from a clothespin!

1 Take a drinking straw and cut off two 1-inch lengths. Straighten two paperclips and thread them through the straws. These are the car's axles.

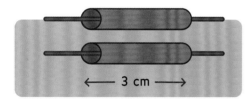
← 3 cm →

2 To make the wheels, lie a milk bottle lid on a blob of sticky tack. Ask an adult to use an awl to punch a hole in the middle of the lid. Remove the sticky tack and repeat.

3 Push the ends of the paperclip wires through the holes in the lids. Bend the ends over with pliers and secure with sticky tape.

4 Place one axle through the hole formed when the clothespin is closed. Secure it with tape. Push the other axle between the clothespin handles and wrap tape around the handles to keep the axle in position.

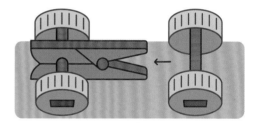

The Science: WHEEL MOVEMENT

As you know from page 33, wheels turn the effort of the turning axle into a greater distance of ground covered. They also reduce the friction with the ground. In this experiment, the car's axles were free to rotate separately from the rest of the car. All wheels and axles work like this.

DID YOU KNOW?

One of the world's biggest wheels is the High Roller Ferris Wheel in Las Vegas, USA. It measures 548 feet tall!

5 Make a sloping surface by propping one end of a board on some books, then set your car whizzing downhill.

Car challenges:

1 Why not build a second car and hold a race down the slope?

2 Your car has no engine. Can you attach an elastic band to your peg car so it can be fired forward like the rocket on pages 44–45?

A LOAD OF HOT AIR

What happens to air when you heat it up?
Find out by making your own hot air balloon!
For launch instructions, turn the page.

WARNING!
1 AN ADULT MUST OPERATE THE HAIR DRYER at step 8!
2 Don't use a hair dryer for more than five minutes or it may overheat.
3 Don't heat just one area of the plastic or it may melt.

ASK AN ADULT

1 Unfold a trash bag and lay it flat on a table. Fold down one of the corners at the closed end and secure it with tape.

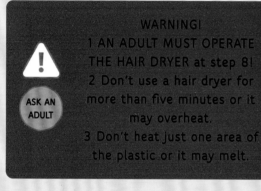

2 Turn the bag over, fold down the other closed corner and stick it down with tape.

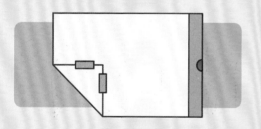

If your bag has a drawstring, go to step 3. If it has handles, jump to step 5.

3 If your bag has a drawstring, simply pull the drawstring so that the opening of the bag narrows to about 6 inches.

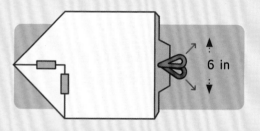

6 in

4 Stick tape over the rim of the drawstring bag and stick the drawstring itself to the side of the bag. Roll the opening back about 1 inch and stick it down with more tape. Now go to step 7.

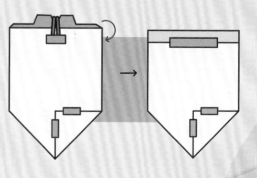

You will need...

- Large trash bag
- Wide tape
- Ruler
- Scissors
- Hair dryer
- Cotton thread
- Balloon
- 2-liter plastic bottle
- 2 bowls
- Ice cubes
- Hot water
- Extension cable

The trash bag should be as lightweight as possible. The type with a drawstring works best.

5 If your bag has handles, cut them off, then fold the opening back about 1 inch. Use tape to stick the fold down across the whole width of the bag.

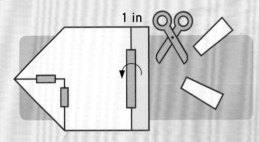

DID YOU KNOW?

The hot air balloon was invented by the Montgolfier brothers in France in 1783.

6 Cut a semicircle through both sides of the bag opening, as shown.

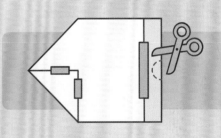

7 Pull the sides of the bag apart to reveal a round hole. Hold the bag upright and allow air to fill it.

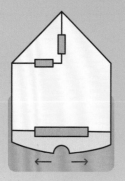

8 Wait for a cool day without wind. When you're outside, take a reel of cotton thread and unroll a length equal to the height you want your balloon to fly. Tape the end of the thread to the base of the bag.

Hot Air challenge 2:

Blow up a balloon and let the air out of it. Roll the neck of the balloon over an empty 2-liter bottle. Fill one bowl with ice cubes and cold water and one with hot water from the tap.

1 Place the bottle in the hot bowl for a few minutes.

2 Then place the bottle in the cold bowl.

3 Repeat steps 1 and 2. Can you explain what happens to the balloon in terms of changes in heat and air pressure?

Answer:
The hot bowl heats the air in the bottle, and it expands, filling the balloon. The cold bowl cools the air, making it contract, and the balloon empties.

ASK AN ADULT

9 Set a hairdryer to its most powerful setting, but don't switch it on yet! Hold the bag, and ask your adult helper to push the end of the hairdryer into the hole. Ask them to switch on the hairdryer and fill the bag with hot air. When the sides of the bag are bulging, release the bag and watch what happens.

⚠ **WARNING!**
Hot-tap water can be very hot. Be careful not to spill it on your hands.

The Science:
AIR, HEAT, AND AIR PRESSURE

When the air in the bag heats up, the sides bulge outwards and the balloon floats up. After a short while, the bag floats down again.

The bag is like a hot air balloon. Air is a mixture of gases: mostly nitrogen and oxygen. When air heats up, the gas molecules get the energy to move apart. This makes air pressure increase. The increase in air pressure causes the sides of the bags to bulge outward.

Some air pushes out from the hole in the base of the bag. The bag occupies a larger volume with less air, and since it's lighter than the same volume of cooler air, the bag floats upward.

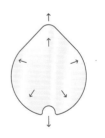

As the air in the bag cools again, the air pressure drops. Cooler air from outside enters the bag and it gets heavier. Gravity pulls the bag back down.

THAT SINKING FEELING

Find out how a submarine works by making one of your own. Unlike the real thing, this one won't cost millions of dollars!

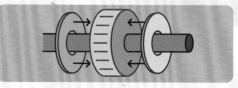

WARNING!
NEVER test your submarine in a pond or any deep water outside.

1 Remove the top from a 2-liter plastic bottle. Ask an adult to cut three ½-inch holes in the side of the bottle with sharp scissors.

ASK AN ADULT

2 Use duct tape to attach a table knife to the bottle above and below the holes. Be careful not to tape over the holes.

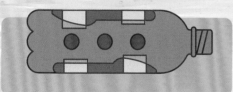

3 Ask an adult to punch a hole through the bottle top with an awl or a nail and hammer. The hole should be the same width as your thin plastic tubing.

ASK AN ADULT

4 Take a 20-inch length of thin plastic tubing and push 1.5 inches down through the hole in the bottle top.

5 Slide a washer onto each end of the tubing. Push the washers along the tubing until they touch the bottle top. Seal the join between the washers and the tubing with sticky tack.

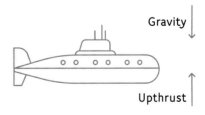

You will need...

- 2 liter screw-top plastic bottle
- Sharp scissors
- Duct tape
- 2 round-end table knives
- Awl or nail and hammer
- 20 inches thin plastic tubing
- Two rubber tap washers
- Masking tape
- Bath full of water

6 Wrap masking tape around the tube below the bottle top. Screw the top onto the bottle. Then wrap duct tape around the neck of the bottle and the sticky tack.

7 Fill a bath and place your submarine in the water. Watch it dive as water enters the holes. To make it rise, just blow through the tube!

The Science: FLOATING AND SINKING

Gravity ↓

Upthrust ↑

The knives that you taped to your submarine make it heavier than its own volume of water. So as it fills with water, it sinks. The force of gravity pulling the submarine down is stronger than the force of the water, called upthrust, that pushes it up.

When you blow air into the submarine, some of the water inside it is pushed out, making the submarine lighter than its volume of water. Upthrust makes it float. Real submarines work in a similar way, by filling and emptying their water tanks.

JETTING OFF!

Jet engines, propellers, and space rockets work on the principle that when air blows backward, they move forward! Test this out by making your own balloon rocket.

1 Place two chairs 16-26 feet apart. Take a ball of string and tie one end to one of the chairs. Measure out enough string to reach the other chair and cut it off.

2 Cut two 1.5-inch lengths of drinking straw and two 1.5-inch lengths of tape. Inflate and deflate a balloon three times to make it baggy.

3 Partly inflate the balloon and ask a friend to pinch the neck to keep the air in. Line up the two straw lengths on the balloon and stick them on with the two pieces of sticky tape.

DID YOU KNOW?

The Laws of Motion discovered by scientist Sir Isaac Newton (1642-1727) explain how everything in the universe moves.

4 Deflate the balloon, thread the free end of the string through the straws, then tie the end of the string to the second chair. Now fully inflate the balloon, and let go!

You will need...

- Two chairs
- Tape measure
- Ball of string
- Scissors
- Drinking straw
- Tape
- Balloon
- Friend helper

The Science:
NEWTON'S LAWS OF MOTION

As the air in the balloon escapes, the balloon whizzes along the string. Isaac Newton's Third Law of Motion explains this. The Law says that for every force, there is an equal and opposite reaction. This means when the air blows backward from the balloon, the balloon moves forward.

Here's what Newton's other two Laws say about the balloon:

First Law: a resting balloon won't move. A moving balloon whizzes in a straight line unless another force affects it.

Second Law: the balloon moves in the direction of the force that moves it. Its acceleration (change of speed) depends on its mass and the strength of the force. An increase in force accelerates the balloon.

Try using different sizes and shapes of balloon. Which sizes or shapes move faster?

Newton's Third Law challenge:

Stand on a skateboard or rollerskates and push against a wall. What happens? Can you explain it in terms of Newton's Third Law?

Answer:
You move away from the wall! This is because your push produces an equal and opposite push back from the wall.

BAKING SODA SPEEDBOAT

Smart engineers don't row boats. They get chemicals to do the hard work!

1 Use a marker to draw a boat shape on a polystyrene pizza base.

2 Cut out the boat shape. Use duct tape to stick a plastic bottletop, open end up, to the front end.

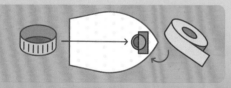

3 Cut and bend two drinking straws and attach them to the boat with duct tape, as shown.

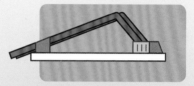

Instead of using duct tape, you could stick a strip of polystyrene across the ends of the straws to hold them in place.

The great baking powder boat race challenge:

Build a second boat and organize a boat race with a friend. Hold a wooden spoon upright in the water to mark the position of the back of the first boat. Add the vinegar and watch it go. When it stops moving, measure the straight-line distance from the wooden spoon to the back of the boat. Then challenge your friend to beat that distance with their boat. Whichever boat travels farthest, wins!

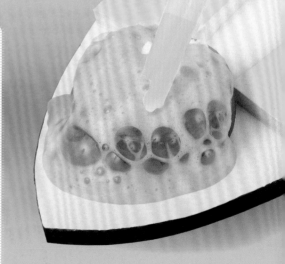

You will need...

- Polystyrene pizza base
- Marker
- Scissors
- Plastic bottle top
- Duct tape
- 2 bendable drinking straws
- Baking powder
- Teaspoon
- Vinegar
- Wooden spoon
- Tape measure

4 Add two teaspoons of baking powder to the lid.

The Science:
NEWTON'S THIRD LAW AND POTENTIAL ENERGY

What happened in the lid is the same chemical reaction we saw take place on page 29. The base in the baking powder reacted with the acid in the vinegar to produce carbon dioxide gas. This time, the carbon dioxide gas was chaneled through the straws and pushed into the water behind the boat. Newton's Third Law of Motion (see page 57) explains how an equal and opposite force then pushed your boat forward.

Just like your elastic-powered rocket (pages 44–45), the energy to power your boat was stored. This time the store wasn't stretchy molecules; it was the two chemicals that combined in the chemical reaction. Rather like the fuel that powers many machines, the two chemicals are an energy store. The proper name for stored energy such as fuel is "potential energy," because it can be used in the future.

5 Fill a bath or sink with water and float your boat. Pour a little vinegar into the lid, and watch what happens!

You could have fun decorating your boat with extra features, such as seats and a flag!

CLEVER CIRCUITS

Circuits carry the vital force that powers all electrical machines. Find out how a simple circuit works...

WARNING!
You MUST use a zinc chloride battery. Other types of battery may overheat.

ASK AN ADULT

1 Take a 12-inch length of electrical wire, and measure and mark a line about a ¼ inch from each end. Ask an adult to strip the plastic covering off the copper wire up to your marker lines.

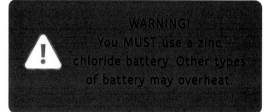

2 Use tape to stick one end of the wire to the base (negative end) of the battery.

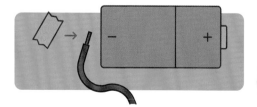

3 Hold the base of a torch bulb against the positive end of the battery. Touch the loose end of the wire to the metal side of the bulb and the bulb will light up!

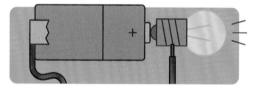

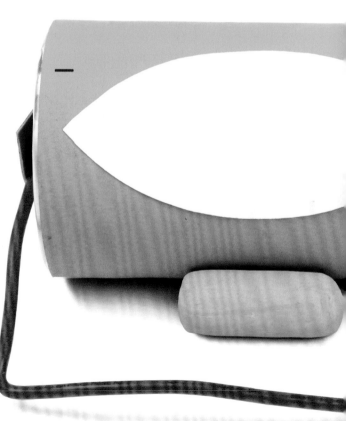

You will need...

- 12 inches electrical wire
- Ruler
- Marker
- Wire strippers
- Tape
- 2 zinc chloride batteries (AA type, 1.5v)
- Flashlight bulb

Instead of a flashlight bulb, you could use a small fridge bulb from a hardware shop.

The Science:
ELECTRICAL CIRCUITS AND SWITCHES

When you touch the end of the wire to the bulb, an electric current flows from the battery to the bulb, through the wire, and back to the battery. The bulb lights as the electric current flows through it.

Electric current can only flow in a circle called an electric circuit—and this explains why your electric current only flows when the battery, wire, and bulb are in contact. Unless everything is in contact the circuit isn't complete. A switch—like a light switch—is a device that controls the flow of electric current. It stops the electric current flowing by breaking the electric circuit.

Electric circuit challenge:

Tape the positive ends of two batteries together. Hold a bulb against the negative end of the second battery and touch the loose end of the wire against its metal side.

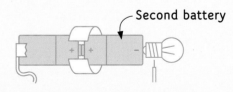

Second battery

1 Why does the electric current not flow now?

2 How can you solve the problem?

Answers:
1. Current only flows from positive to negative.
2. Reverse a battery so positive touches negative.

WIND POWER

Wind has been powering windmills for centuries, and it's used to make electricity, too. What will engineers use it for in the future? Here's how to make a windmill that lifts things (see page 65)...

1 Ask an adult to stick a sharp pencil through a plastic bottle from one side to the other.

At step 1, your adult helper might need to start the hole with a nail. The hole must go in a straight line.

2 Take a straight straw (not the bendy type) and push it through the holes. Trim the ends of the straw so they stick out 1 inch from the sides of the bottle.

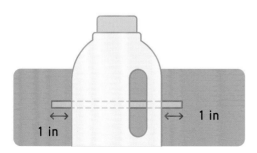

1 in   1 in

3 Push a thin wooden dowel or barbecue skewer through the straw so that it sticks out of the straw 3-4 inches on one side and ½ inch on the other. You may need to cut the dowel to the right length.

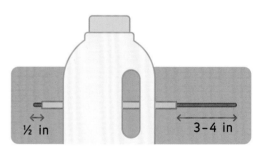

½ in   3-4 in

4 Cut out a 2.5-inch wide circle from thick cardstock. Cut a 1 inch slot every 120°, as shown—use a protractor to measure the angles.

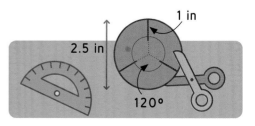

1 in

2.5 in

120°

62

You will need...

- Sharp pencil
- Plastic bottle
  (4 pint milk bottle
  is ideal)
- Straight straw
- Scissors
- Ruler
- Thin wooden dowel
  or barbecue skewer
- Thick cardstock
- Protractor
- Drawing pin
- Marker
- Thin plastic
- or cardstock
- Tape
- String
- Sticky tack
- Hairdryer

You can buy thin dowel from DIY or craft shops. It must be thin enough to fit through the straw.

5 Use a drawing pin to attach the circle to the short end of the dowel, as shown.

6 Draw a blade shape on some cardstock or thin plastic and cut it out. Use this blade as a template to make two more blades the same size and shape.

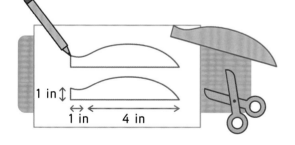

1 in
1 in   4 in

7 Roll each blade around a pencil to give it a curved shape.

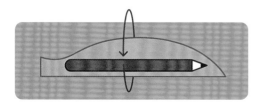

8 Push the thin ends of the blades into the slots in your cardstock circle. Make sure the curved sides are all pointing the same way.

9 Cut a 16-inch length of string. Use tape to attach one end of the string to the long end of the dowel. Attach a small blob of sticky tack to the loose end of the string as a weight.

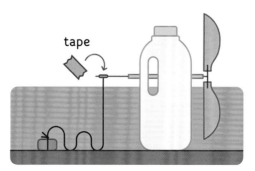

tape

10 Your windmill is ready for testing. Set a hairdryer to low power and point it at the blades. Air blowing from the hairdryer turns the blades, and this makes the dowel rotate. As it turns, it winds the string and lifts the weight!

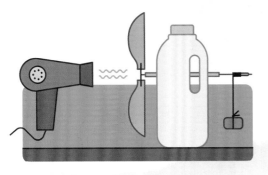

Wind turbine challenge:

Move the hairdryer closer to the blades, then move it farther away. How does the distance between the hairdryer and the blades affect the speed at which the machine winds the string? Why does the distance make a difference?

Draw and make three sets of different-shaped blades for your windmill. Are they any better or worse at winding the string? How could you set up a fair test to compare them with your first set of blades?

The Science: ELECTRICITY GENERATION

Wind is simply moving air. When it's very strong, it has lots of energy. Like your windmill, a wind turbine uses the energy of moving air to turn blades, which turn a shaft. Instead of a string, in a wind turbine the shaft powers a generator to make electricity.

On pages 46–47, you used an electric current to move a magnet. But you can also use a magnet to get an electric current moving. Inside a generator, the shaft turns a wire. The wire is in a strong magnetic field. As the wire moves, an electric current flows through it.

Thousands of engineers are working to build or improve wind turbines for the future. The good thing about this technology is that wind energy is free and never runs out of puff!

DID YOU KNOW?

In 2019 engineers were planning to erect a 853-foot tall wind turbine—that's nearly twice the height of the Great Pyramid in Egypt—with a rotor circle of 722 feet in diameter.

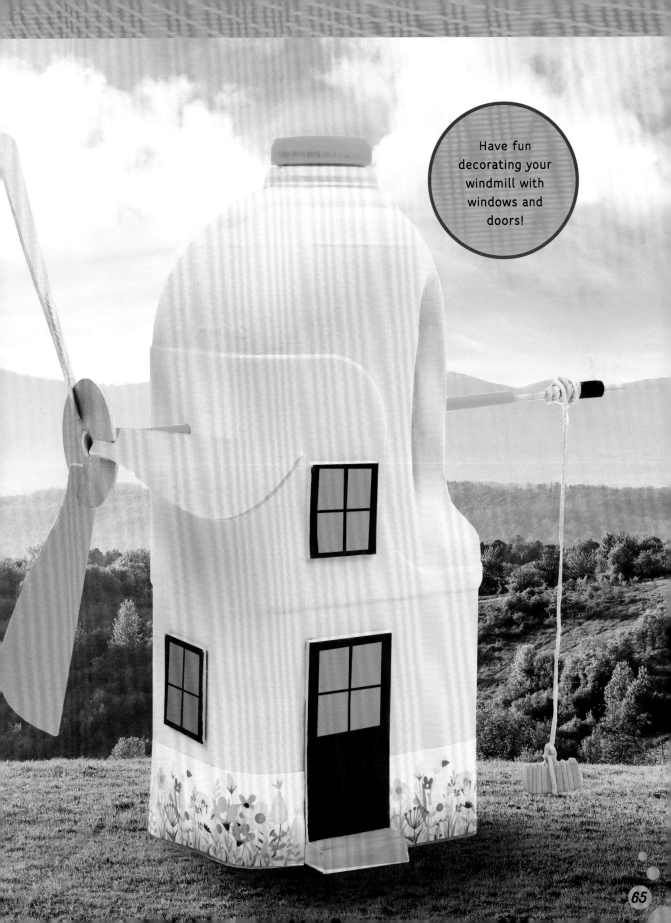

Have fun decorating your windmill with windows and doors!

THE FUTURE FOR CROPS!

The world's population just keeps on growing, and that means more people to feed. One way to tackle this is to grow crops without soil...

1 Ask an adult to cut a plastic bottle in half across the middle.

ASK AN ADULT

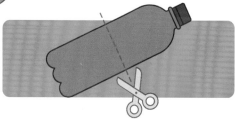

3 Put the cotton wool balls into the bottom half of the bottle.

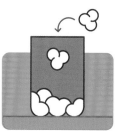

2 Fill a small bowl with water. Dip 20-30 cotton wool balls in the water. Squeeze them if necessary so they are moist but not soaking wet.

4 Scatter some cress seeds over the cotton wool balls.

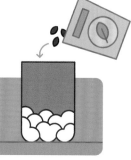

The Science:
HYDROPONIC AGRICULTURE

Your experiment shows that soil ISN'T vital for plants! As long as their roots are supported and they have the right amount of moisture and minerals, plants can grow happily.

Growing plants without soil is called hydroponics. Farmers use this system to grow food in places where there is a shortage of land for crops, or where conditions are very dry. By very precisely controlling the amount of plant food and water they give to their crops, farmers are able to get the most produce from their plants.

You will need...

- Clean 2-liter plastic bottle with screw top
- Scissors
- Small bowl
- Water
- 20–30 cotton wool balls
- Cress seeds
- Wide tape

5 Use wide tape to join the top half of the bottle to the bottom half.

6 Leave the bottle for a few days. The cress seeds will sprout in 24–48 hours, and the stems will be ready to pick and eat in 5–7 days.

If your cotton wool balls are too moist, you can dry them by opening the lid for a few hours. If they're too dry, add a little water.

DID YOU KNOW?

In 2018, engineers built a hydroponic farm in Dubai that is able to grow 5.3 tons of green vegetables EVERY DAY!

MARBLE MAYHEM

Tomorrow's engineers won't just be thinking about serious stuff. They'll be designing fun things, too. Give some fun engineering a try...

1 Take a large cardboard box and cut off the flaps. Make a hole in the top big enough for a bottle neck.

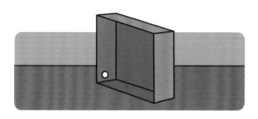

2 Design a marble run on paper. Mark where you'd like the pipes, funnels, and gulleys to go (see below).

Marble run design:

Tape gulleys, funnels, and pipes to the inside of the box, leading down to a small box where the marbles are caught. The design is up to you!

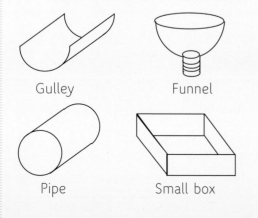

Gulley

Funnel

Pipe

Small box

3 To make a gulley, cut a toilet or paper towel roll in half lengthways.

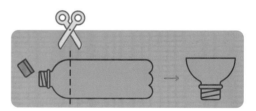

4 To make a funnel, cut off the top part of a plastic bottle.

The Science:
GRAVITY AND FRICTION

The force of gravity pulls the marbles down the slopes. Friction slows them down. Without friction, the marbles would get to the bottom faster.

You will need...

- Large cardboard box
- Scissors
- Pencil and paper
- 4 or more toilet or paper towel tubes
- Large plastic bottles
- Small box
- Marbles
- Tape

5 When you have made all your gulleys, pipes, and funnels, assemble your design.

6 Don't forget to stick down a small box to catch the marbles.

7 Test your marble run!

Make sure the neck of the bottle you use for a funnel is wide enough for your marbles to fit through.

CRAZY CODE

There's a secret code that makes computers clever. Can you write it and read it? Try using it to send secret messages to a friend!

1 Ask a friend to write a secret message, and write one yourself. Don't show each other! Keep your messages short—ideally no more than 26 letters.

2 Next, both of you need to draw this grid on a sheet of paper.

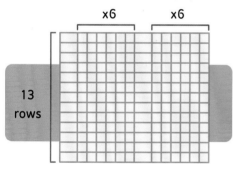

x6   x6

13 rows

3 Both repeat step 2 on a second sheet of paper.

4 Now both of you need to copy out the code reader below onto one of your grid sheets.

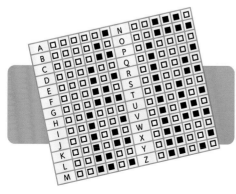

5 Move apart so you can't see each other's paper, and both use your code reader to encode your message on your blank grid. Write the code for the first letter in the top row of the left-hand column, and work down letter by letter. Don't leave gaps between words. Then move on to the second column. For each square, where there's a black blob on the code reader, use the point of your pen to make a hole in the paper big enough to see through.

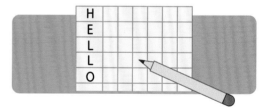

6 Swap code sheets with your friend. Move their code sheet over your code reader grid. When a six-square letter code is on top of the correct letter, you'll see black through all its holes. Write the letter in the left-hand margin of the code sheet.

7 Write out the decoded message. Swap the decoded message with your friend. Did you get it right?

You will need...

- Friend
- 6 sheets of paper
- Pen
- Ruler
- Felt pen

At step 2, you could use a photocopier to print out several enlarged copies of the grid.

SECRET DECODER
AGENT NAME:

A					
B					
C					

SECRET MESSAGE

The Science:
BINARY CODE AND SOFTWARE

The programs and operating information used by computers are called software. Computer software is based on binary code. This is a pattern of 1's and 0's that controls the computer. Computers also store information in the form of binary code.

ASCII (American Standard Computer Information Interchange) is a binary code for letters and other characters that you type with a keyboard. In this project, you used the last six digits of ASCII letters to code your message (the first two are always the same). You used a black square for 1 and a white square for 0.

Code challenge:

Can you decode your message faster than your friend?

71

HOW TO TRAIN A ROBOT

Robotic engineers are designing the next generation of robots. Here's how to control a robot of your own...

1 Make a glass of your favorite drink and place it in a room, perhaps on a chair or table.

2 Measure the length and width of the room in feet. Then draw a corresponding grid on a sheet of paper: 1 square = 1 square foot. Color in the squares where there are items of furniture.

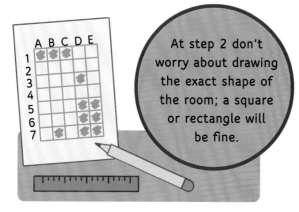

At step 2 don't worry about drawing the exact shape of the room; a square or rectangle will be fine.

3 Mark sticky labels with the reference of each square—for example A1, A2, and so on, and place the sticky labels in the correct positions on the floor of the room.

4 Which square will your robot start from? Mark this square on your grid. Mark your position and the position of the drink on your grid.

5 Look at the Robot Control Code example. Write your own Robot Control Code that will take your robot to the drink, pick it up, and bring it to you.

6 Your friend is the robot. Don't tell them what you want. Give them your Robot Control Code and ask them to follow the instructions. Can they do it?

Robot control code

🤖 = Robot   ↑ = Up
& = Move   ↓ = Down
G = Grab or give   → = Right
☑ = Drink   ← = Left

Example instruction
In this example, the robot starts in square A3, the drink is in square E2, and you are in square C7. The arrow directions refer to movements on the grid.

🤖&↑A2&→E2G☑ &←C2&↓C7G☑

You will need...

- Glass of your favorite drink
- A big room
- Tape measure
- Paper
- Pencil
- Sticky labels
- Felt pen
- Friend

Robot challenge:

Make a model robot from scrap materials, such as:
· Large and small cardboard boxes and corrugated cardboard
· Toilet roll tubes
· Plastic bottle lids

The Science:
ALGORITHMS

Just like a computer, a robot is a machine controlled by binary code. In this project, you wrote an algorithm—a set of software instructions that can be turned into binary code. Software engineers write algorithms to control robots, computers, and lots of other digital devices.

DID YOU KNOW?

Algorithms control internet search engines. It is estimated that Google's search engines perform 63,000 searches every second!

SPACE TO LIVE

Will people in the future live in space stations up in space or on other planets? Find out what it's like to be a space engineer by building your very own out-of-this-world space station!

1 Take an empty aluminum foil box and ask an adult to carefully peel off the cutting strip. Stick down the flap using double-sided tape.

ASK AN ADULT

2 Cut holes on opposite sides of the box, as shown. The holes should be very slightly narrower than a paper towel tube. Paint the box white.

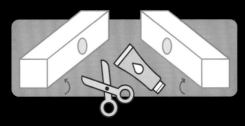

3 Paint two paper towel tubes white.

4 Stand one of the tubes on a piece of cardstock and draw around the end. Add four flaps. Cut out the shape, fold the flaps over, and glue them to the inside of the tube. Repeat with the other tube.

> **MESS WARNING!**
> Put down newspaper and wear old clothes.

5 Ask an adult to cut two 1-inch slits opposite each other at each end of the box. Push the paper towel tubes into the holes by gently squeezing the ends.

ASK AN ADULT

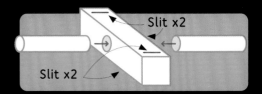

Slit x2

Slit x2

6 Cut two 12-inch strips of cardboard and paint black rectangles on both sides. These are the solar panels.

7 Push the solar panels through the slits in the box.

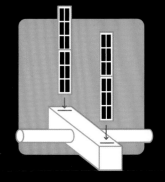

If you don't have acrylic paints, you could cover the box and tubes with white paper.

DID YOU KNOW?

The temperature in space is -454.81 °F—almost as cold as it's possible to be. But direct sunlight would burn your skin!

The Science: SPACE ENGINEERING

Like your model, real space stations are made up of units that are fitted together. They need to be lightweight so they can be transported by a rocket. Spacecraft move the large sections together, and astronauts bolt on small sections. The materials used must be able to withstand extreme heat AND extreme cold. The solar panels are used to make electricity.

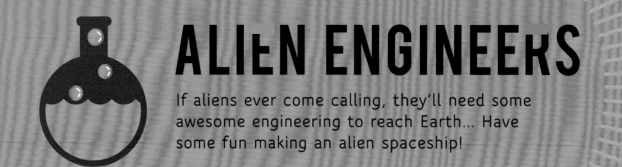

ALIEN ENGINEERS

If aliens ever come calling, they'll need some awesome engineering to reach Earth... Have some fun making an alien spaceship!

1 Screw up a sheet of waste paper and push it between two paper plates. Staple the plates together around the edges.

2 Take a paper bowl and draw a 2-inch wide circle on its base. Cut out the circle. Push a clear plastic cup up through the hole from underneath.

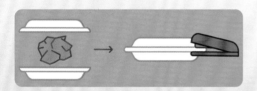

3 Paint a cardstock alien or make one from modeling clay and put it in the cup.

4 Glue the bowl to the upside-down paper plate.

5 Decorate your alien spacecraft!

DID YOU KNOW?

Apart from the Sun, our nearest star is Proxima Centauri. It would take 19,000 years to fly there in a spacecraft.

You will need...

- Waste paper
- 2 paper plates
- Stapler
- Paper bowl
- Pencil
- Ruler
- Scissors
- Clear plastic cup
- Modeling clay
- Cardstock
- Paints
- Glue
- Pens or stickers to decorate
- String
- Tape

6 Cut a length of string and tape it to the plastic cup. Hang up your alien spacecraft so it hovers in mid-air.

The Science:
ALIEN ENGINEERING

Our galaxy contains millions of planets where aliens might live. But don't panic! The planets are a long way off, and we haven't met any aliens yet. Any alien spacecraft would need to be:

· Fast enough to reach other planets
· Strong enough to withstand conditions in space
· Big enough to carry everything an alien needs

The final word:
ENGINEERING SCIENCE

Engineers are "can-do" people! Whatever you want—be it a new building, a new machine, or even a new invention—engineers make it happen. To help them, engineers use science. For them, science isn't just a school subject; it's a guide that explains everything they do. In the future, the world will need more engineers to design and build all kinds of different things. Could you be one of them? Why not dream up your some engineering experiments of your own so you're ready to take on the future!

GLOSSARY

Acid – a type of chemical. When mixed with water, strong acids can dissolve other substances.

Air pressure – the force of the air pressing on an object.

Binary code – a series of 1's and 0's that store information or control a computer–1 is a set amount of electricity and 0 is nothing.

Chemical reaction – when two or more chemicals combine to make a new chemical. Some chemical reactions can be reversed and others can't.

Digital machine – a machine controlled by on-off code–often binary code. Digital machines include smart phones and digital cameras.

Electric current – flow of electric charge in a circle called a circuit. Charge is a quality of particles such as electrons.

Electromagnetism – electric and magnetic force produced by moving charged particles.

Energy – what you need to move an object a distance using force. Energy has many forms including heat and movement. It often changes form.

Fair test – test with one detail altered. The experiment shows the effect of altering this detail.

Friction – rubbing force produced between moving surfaces or a moving surface in contact with gas or liquid. Friction slows moving objects.

Gravity – force produced by matter pulling on other matter. The pull of gravity on an object can be measured by weighing it.

Magnetic field – area affected by a magnetic force. Iron filings sprinkled over a magnet reveal its magnetic field.

Machine – a device that changes the direction and strength of a force in order to achieve a particular result.

Mass – all the matter in an object. Any object that contains atoms has mass.

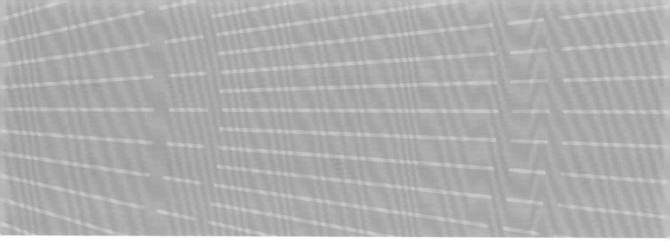

Molecule – group of atoms bonded together. Most chemicals consist of molecules.

Momentum – ability of a moving object to keep moving. Objects with lots of mass and speed have more momentum than lighter, slower objects.

Solar panel – device using sunlight energy to make an electric current.

Tectonic plate – vast slabs of rock forming the Earth's outer layer or crust. The plates slowly move–powered by churning currents of melted rock.

Water pressure – force caused by the weight of water pressing on an object. The force is equal in all directions.

INDEX